Graves Too Small to Be Red

poems by

Laura Cini English

Finishing Line Press
Georgetown, Kentucky

Graves Too Small to Be Red

Copyright © 2018 by Laura Cini English
ISBN 978-1-63534-460-8 First Edition
All rights reserved under International and Pan-American Copyright Conventions.
No part of this book may be reproduced in any manner whatsoever without written permission from the publisher, except in the case of brief quotations embodied in critical articles and reviews.

ACKNOWLEDGMENTS

Cider Press Review ~ Story
Connecticut River Review ~ Moving Days
Off the Coast ~ Found on the Road
Pudding Magazine ~ Small Footprints
Common Ground Review ~ In the Center

Publisher: Leah Maines
Editor: Christen Kincaid
Cover Art: Rogan English
Author Photo: Garrick English
Cover Design: Elizabeth Maines McCleavy

Printed in the USA on acid-free paper.
Order online: www.finishinglinepress.com
         also available on amazon.com

              Author inquiries and mail orders:
                  Finishing Line Press
                    P. O. Box 1626
              Georgetown, Kentucky 40324
                       U. S. A.

Table of Contents

Story 1

Moving Days 2

Mocoa, Colombia 3

Found on the Road 4

Small Footprints 5

Water 6

Red All Over 7

Instead 8

A Two-Year-Old Writes a Letter to Himself on His
    Birthday When He Comes of Age 9

Children Going Home 10

In the Center 11

Sounds Like 12

Junco 13

Not Sure If Angels Will Follow 14

North Has a Closer Sun 15

How Liza Pollack and John Scordato Scored 17

Portrait 18

Isaiah in the Wilderness 19

The Job You Were Given 21

The Instruction 22

Children Raised in the Temple 23

Diastasis Recti 24

Finding a Place for It 25

That Slip of Light When Clouds Move Apart Briefly 26

The Spare Room 27

In memory of the one who played under the apple tree

Story

Before the signal hits midnight clouds,
Batman's on the bridge

putting his arms around the frenzied father,
guiding madness into two magic rings.

An officer helps the girl down from the rail
and wraps her in wings his mother knitted.

Then there's the cottage in an enchanted forest,
a nice couple who always wanted a little girl.

They buy her a blue dress and a Dora lunch box.
The whole village cheers, sends roses

and a tray of sweet cakes. She forgets
her real father, marries a handsome prince.

Now she's queen of a distant land, where jelly beans
grow on trees. She rules with utter kindness.

When a baby is born, spells are cast
that the father never overwhelm his child.

We tell this to her classmates in kindergarten
who ask why her seat is empty.

We tell it to the fear that hangs over the bay
and birds won't fly into.

Moving Days

It was my job on moving day to hold doors open
        and not to lift
because I was small, because I was a girl, I would get underfoot,
        my arms weren't strong.
Because I weighed far less than the object being moved,
        sleeper sofa, bookcase, my mother's upright piano,
I wished the burdens lighter, and hoped by my wishing
        the movers would find strength.
Pressed against the wall, I held my breath, imagined
        a real assignment when I grew powerful.

Like yesterday when I read in a box within a box on the screen
        of someone's son, machete
through his neck on the way to school, same age
        as my third child.
I wanted to be at the controls of a time machine, a chopper
        that would scoop up the boy
before the gang surrounded him, and take him to a country
        where people afford paper towels and pet food.
Instead I am told there is already a guide leading
        the dead to calmer places.
I am to stay behind and tend the door for sorrow as it goes
        from one side to another.

Some grief is large as a wardrobe built inside the house
        board by board. It is hard to pass
as a house through a house. A man once built an airplane
        in his attic, forgetting the way out.
Shaped like a cross, it needed to be dismantled bolt by bolt
        and reassembled carefully before it could lift.

Mocoa, Colombia

We never woke up Saturday morning,
the rain chiseling the mountain into quick graves.

A list of our names pinned to a board. Our parents'
nightclothes and hair permeated with mud.

You groped for me when you woke,
remembering I had gone to bed close to you.

You don't have to wade through filth up to your waist,
stretching out your arms as if blindfolded.

Think of me growing older than you, the age of stones.
I am your parent and godparent and great-grandfather.

Go. Volunteers are passing out something to eat.
Drinking water runs out of the drum, and

your tears will also exhaust themselves.
Remember when I was buried

in your body. You had to move with heaviness.
Remember how you loved what was hidden. Don't dream

a tiny boat swallowed by the ocean.
Dream of a seabird that scatters its weight across the surface.

When happiness comes to the village again like a young man
swinging a hammer, maybe it will find you

among the splintered roofs and overturned trucks,
and police bearing children who are not yours on their backs.

Listen to me— let yourself be found,
as a drunk is found by the sun of a new day.

Found on the Road

The blonde girl in the news that was supposed to die,
both arms slashed by an attacker
and her friends dead on the ground beside her.
The reporter steels. What can be done?

Yet she appears the way an angel
enters a Dutch room full of light,
shows up in our town's school
this Wednesday afternoon.

She descends the stairs
on the shoulders of the crowd
like a surfer on a wave.
A glimpse of her wounds, they

are pale lips, closing. How does
her sleeveless dress flutter green?
In the back of a classroom, she stays
awake. We ask forgiveness in our hearts

for having doubted her survival
as the clock ticks her into present tense.
A boy in tattoos confesses
he has loved her for years, tenderly

kisses her cheek, and the town follows
his lead. We love her at once,
bringing fine gifts as if from other planets.
A man offers the blanket of his childhood.

We choose her a slim book—
with a happy ending!
Each of us a lit candle around her body,
her Samaritan eyes upon us.

Small Footprints

stretching across the roof,
from one side to the other.

Like a fox in a cathedral,
fur singed on fires of the Holy Spirit,

a child touched the high,
blue electric while we lay sleeping.

I whisper names of lost ones
to the west wind. No answer comes.

My hands open like a newspaper
telling about a boy without a name.

Black and white flits distracted
like a magpie. A shift

of tail feathers, now green, sometimes blue,
and the imagination speaks what no one will.

His skin in shreds, face unwashed, sound
of thick tape unrolling as his mother

pinned his thighs. I nudge you through morning,
ask, are you going to drink

the coffee or watch it trembling in your cup?
Oh, inconsolable life, even the meteorites.

I love your mess of vengeance and grief.
In your dreams you broke down the door,

beat the mother and boyfriend bloody. I dimly see
what you did in secret beneath your waking.

You were the stranger who stayed with him
in uncharted space. He has come back to dismiss you.

Water

It remains on the street after a child is stripped
and hosed to wash his body of poison
fallen from the sky over a town where rebels hide.

People like you and me walk through it later,
on our way to buy a newspaper.

It gets on the soles of the shoe, and leaves footprints
leading away from the shouts and cries of the morning.

Dogs lap it up and would foam at the mouth,
and struggle for breathe the way the boy did
except enough of it has mixed with the venom.

No one will do anything
that can bring back the dead.
In the afternoon the sun lifts it into the sky,

and when it floats high enough, the wind takes it.
It comes back as rain. It falls as far-away snow.

It ought to find its way into the buried lakes of Antarctica.
It enters instead a bowl of soup, a field, the constitution

of a bystander who has stopped
believing that anything can be pure.

Red All Over

Isn't it red what we wanted to say to defend ourselves
        and thought of a day later?

Red, what we discovered we could have done ourselves
        and not had to give the repairman a week's pay.

Isn't it red, the strawberry I saved when you refused to eat,
        the sun at the end of the day though we wanted it to stay gold?

Isn't it red this madness we feel when the hour is ours
        but with many letters to answer?

Red, this feeling of getting older, our hands tied,
        time fastening a belt around us.

Isn't the stoplight red, and who thought of that
        when red is the color for charging bulls?

Isn't it red the girl who finds a wolf instead of an older version of herself,
        her basket of biscuits strewn in the red light of the pines?

Isn't it staining the sheets when the tiny life
        won't breathe?

Isn't the water red by some miracle,
        someone suggesting a bloom of algae?

Isn't it clear when a bullet stops
        a quarrel?

Red where someone's birthday
        should have been circled on the calendar.

Put it in print
        where it can be read without pain.

Instead

"[throw]
        the five-year-old down
the cellar stairs for urinating in his pants."

It was what the newspaper said. It had already happened.

        If electricity brakes
runaway trains, and something tiny as the teeth of mice
        breaks circuits, we stop the arc of fire inside
a frustrated step-father instead of saying, how terrible.

        All we can think of to do is break
down the door of the house and shake the man.

The impulse belongs to his hands where we can't reach it
        through ordinary means. Where time curves

        he is always
about to open the cellar door

and we are always too late
        or lazy
about our own ticks, obsessions, losses of reason.

It has to do with the little bit in him
        connected to the little bit in us.

A piece of atom on one side of the universe, long
        ago torn off from the main,
signals when the other part changes trillions of miles away.

This is unbelievable but true.

Redemption is not for the skeptical.

When you lay the newspaper aside, shaking your head,
        he opens the cellar door.

A Two-Year-Old Writes a Letter to Himself on His Birthday When He Comes Of Age

By now someone will have told you what happened.

The newspaper clipping will have been unearthed, consulted, words
written by someone who didn't know you, and could say it
    like reciting the Pledge of Allegiance or telling a bad joke.

As if I never existed in your life.
As if I were taken away from you the day the police
    cuffed your father.

    She was arms that held me and dark hair.
She put my hand on her belly.
"Imagine a little person inside another."

Truth can be unbelievable.

    He said she was the queen bee.
She was going to destroy the earth.

More than one thing can be true, looking through faceted eyes.

If you "never remember," it's "better that way."

I'm here to tell you the sooner you find a place where everyone belongs—

where giant queen bees and mothers,
and heroes with vintage swords, and baby sisters,
    and fathers with crazed looks live

side by side, the sooner you enter it yourself, and die
    to that inexplicable rage,

the sooner you slip one soul into your body. There must be

    some motel hovering over the grass that maps don't show,
beyond the tangle of forest, off the tired road, a long way from any town,

    a place that even God doesn't know about.
Walls impartial as a womb that gather you in and let you sleep.

Children Going Home

        Released, immortal, immersed
in their shouts and laughing, ditching scarves,
the sun collapsing
snowbanks into rivulets on the lot,
a muscular blue
thinning the sap
moon, they came out into the world again.

Yellow tape hadn't stretched its caution yet
where sirens would accompany a boy's crossing
who was frequently lost
in class, a patient woman at his side.

In a mother's thoughts, he
was approaching the house,
carrying his backpack as always.

The window appeared whole
as if it could never shatter.

It was always after the moment and always before,

even as candles and toys accumulated on the curb,
and snow clung to the hill outside of town,
and stories ran wild
about what caused the driver

not to see. Only the geese coming back
remembered the yoke of the infinite.
In their work, they felt the wind
erase their arrows. They wrote
the lines again.
North was already in them.

In the Center

Garrick, we can't get to the turtles,
the way we can't get through to your brother.

The water rises deeper than our boots,
its surface impenetrable like skin

of green apples, glowing billiards
in the basket. At night the lake piles

on layers of glass. The apples protect
themselves from our hunger.

There are many ways to be hungry,
loneliness at not connecting thoughts

to words, molecules missing their bonds.
So many layers of glass like sweaters

of a person who doesn't want to be touched.
The streetlights shine with knife-like brilliance.

They cut the lake in the center and sink
to depths where the turtles have retreated.

We must keep getting through to your brother.
It was no use wading, rolling our pant legs,

that slippery marching. I wonder if we were
intended to capture what lives in shells.

Only the light enters.
The flesh inside the apple is for travelers

who give their hungers to another world.
Your brother sits on the caked ground

in the center of the jungle
gym, bright as a God's eye.

Sounds Like

When you don't have a place,
it helps to wear a hat you can live under like your own domain.

God discovers nothing except vicariously.

For Him it's a delight
to see us plotting streets and rivers on paper.

I have a desire to look at a diagram
of my son's thoughts if such a thing could be drawn.

A woman who came to
the house taught him to say words with his hands.

In stories of great interpreters, they leave
out the part where the guide drags

the other by the hand
pointing and pronouncing names of objects with rage.

Charades are practice for living in the meantime.

I'll sketch what corresponds
to the country of flight when he flaps his hands.

Heroes are people who constantly live
in the region of meantime.

Junco
evening of Sandy Hook

In the threshold dark, I hear the
doorknob turn. I don't know if I see him
first or the black and white bird
he carries by the tail, trailed
by his younger brother,
pressing into the warmth
past piles of mail and strewn toys.

A wild thing is seldom this close.
It hangs completely still,
its breast, the inside white of roses.
Its legs are pale laces
ending in four aglets each.

How did he find it whole—
not diseased or crushed by tires?
Its eyes shine ice-black in the light of the kitchen
where I wash dirt from potatoes.

Has he brought it in to mend a wing?
Maybe a shoe box and a spot by the fire.
But, no—a hole the size of a seed
fills with dark fluid beneath its beak.

What he meant to kill was a sparrow.
There are too many of them
taking the food of other birds.
He calls this mercy,
the precision of the shot.

Not Sure If the Angels Will Follow

Marcel is about to not be a boy anymore.

His birthday comes on Christmas.

School will keep him a few more years, his teacher walking
    him to lunch.

In August a flood took two buffalo that lived in the zoo.

They couldn't climb to dry land.

Marcel is large with wide eyes and a tiny voice like Charlemagne's.

Teachers and janitors stop what they're doing to greet him.

When he's gone, no one will remind them how to be deliberate
    when doing a simple task.

Their keepers shot them with drugs to let them die
    before the water covered them.

Some days you're called to choose between mercy and the way
    that gives you no blame.

There was news footage, emptiness and then a nest of cranes.

North Has a Closer Sun

        You write to me again about the snow,
another way of saying you belong
where I wouldn't take a step
without sinking into your tracks.
        In the kitchen, one of the onions
unwinds its green measure toward the window.
I had wanted to cook it with red chilies,
waiting for the right craving,
the right moment, like when I
have something to say that would burn
my tongue.
        The awful reaching out,
the lust for the closest star,
how the onion refuses to die
as Christ refused flesh at the end.
Some resurrections leave us
a ladder made of mercy. Yours
left telephone bills, Western
Union, books *Abuela* packed away.
        They say you stepped off
the bus on your way home to see your baby girl.
In their stories you refer to me as a beautiful toy.
Why didn't anyone see the men
who tied the hood, took your daylight?
        After they found you hollow-cheeked
and filthy, they say your mind
kept straying and you followed it,
like a river across the continent.
Barns you slept in, a driver who shaved
while he changed gears of his truck.
When you tore off your old
life and crumpled it like a map,
the names of places no longer true,
you handed my mother a photograph.

        You were a face in the airport
at Christmastime detaching from the crowd.
You were a book of poems
in the mail dedicated
to a woman named Sally, blond
in the pictures I drew in my head.
        Every time they let you up
for air, you told yourself
you could hold on even longer,
the rifle bringing you to your knees
at the trough where pigs drank.
The problem of not saying what
a desperate man wants to hear,
        the hassle of this onion, which belongs
in the ground instead of a basket. My tendency
to let things die, books collect dust, and crosses
of palm bleach and whither.
Where you are, the ground is frozen.
You call it the obstinacy of the Yankee.
Even if a person wanted,
she could not open a hole in the dirt
and let a growing thing go.
Here, winterless, I have no excuse.
I dig into myself, touch stone.
How can I begrudge a green shoot
that splits the air, belongs to no one?

How Liza Pollack and John Scordato Scored

Let wind cross wire and never get cut.
       To be like that
as children tearing our drawings,
and the grown-ups
saying nothing to stop us.
       It was as though our trees had no chance
of packing themselves away
into black seeds, well formed, indestructible.
       A drop of water, a parachute. Down
where the lockers ended, a boy called Devil
would hold his girl until the bell lifted them
to class, lines of desks, and no one in the halls.
       Like Devil, we wedged love
into backseats and dark corners,
curfews taking passion like breath
to a match.
       We would have considered Scordato
lucky, getting it whenever he wanted,
reclining afterward on a soft bed.
Had we known. Had we seen it
before she was sent away to live with her mother.
       Under the same roof, the two of them,
their families fitted together
like broken glass after the reception.
       The book she carried with her—
we couldn't place her in the plot, the brother
and sister who fall in love, the roof
they climb like branches over a garden.
       In school they kept to their circles,
seldom speaking to each other. Something old
and wise in them protected us
       from a third body that dissolved
when morning came and they went out
together to the bus as two children
untangled from their dreams,
the hard work of fog beginning again as wellspring.

Portrait

The photographer went from house to house looking
    for firstborns.

She was a child herself, bony under her robe.

Rags were stuffed between the casing and the window.

Looking back, she never remembered hunger but what there was
    instead of food.

The manger left empty until Christmas was to trick her
    into putting off the good life.

A woman from church had sewn a little blanket from scraps.

Until he was born, she had no champion.

The portrait had to be taken before the glow of infancy
    left his skin.

She had handfuls of change, and milk and bread and whatever

was on lay-away could wait.

A god among us deserves to be anointed.

She ran to get his hat as if he were going somewhere far away.

Isaiah in the Wilderness

We didn't deserve to come this far, listening to the wrong gods,

and our children carrying private altars.

They say Isaiah had the hardest job, a nation
        that wouldn't turn, armies buzzing on the horizon.

Sometimes he didn't think of himself as a person but a river
        flooding its banks, closer to houses, fish in the gardens.

"Master your rage," he used to tell himself, the babies reaching
        for fire, spilling water, tearing the bread.

Then he'd go out of the house and turn his face to the sky.

I would pity one object, and it would be the cross, but it turned to gold.

To hear God's voice one has to become a lesser being.

When we have prophets again, they'll say that their ancestors
        could listen only to idols,

the way children put their ears to broken telephones.

What scientists build in the desert to listen to cold stars—

you can't think of anything more painful.

Most nights I don't clear my mind enough to let in dreams
        untainted by the day's events.

To hold the word of God one empties oneself without being hollow.

When light broke through, it didn't come in syllables
        but an intense drumming on his brain.

Fire touched his lips, and it was a relief.

An object in agony deserves a dream
	to see past invasion to trees that clap their hands.

The Job You Were Given

Will tomorrow be a better day?
Will you go off to do the job you thought you were given?

To be a midwife delivering a baby on a farm.
To start out with aspirations.

A newborn, and the first to touch her soft head.
To be the ambassador to a planet sometimes hostile.

To be a teacher and a bridge,
of letters and numbers, the children as travelers
and you, who will lead them over a chasm of ignorance.

To be a fisherman
and bring up a net wriggling with life
where before there was deep nothingness.

You started your job the day you divided in two.
One is not what you expected.

To throw your body between the Amish man and his wife
so he can't take her after the placenta passes.

To write a report on a child who has picked up his desk
and slammed it into the head of a smaller child.

To keep your boat in the shadow of giant trawlers.

Tomorrow won't be better, but another
glimpse of a holy stranger wearing your clothes.

The Instruction

They've paid the hospital with money from God, multiplied
      by neighbors, packed in brown bags
           like ears of corn in July.

For the long distance, elders have allowed travel by bus
      instead of horse and buggy
           to bring them to the lobby.

She, in a sable bonnet. He, a brim and beard following
      signs to cardiothoracic surgery.
           She holds a baby

wrapped in quilts. They move like foreigners
      not as if from another country
           but a dimension, centuries

apart from the people in the hallways who carry
      purses and backpacks, hurrying.
           They walk as if through a rain

that doesn't touch them. Meeting the secretary's
      gaze, they see that she is wary.
           "The baby has not breathed

since the night before," the father explains gently.
      His face is young and empty
           of song, pale, ancient,

patient with her bewilderment. "Doctor said come
      again to see him if anything
           went wrong with the baby."

Children Raised in the Temple

Kierkegaard could see in Abraham a woman weaning her child.

When we sent our neighbor to the hospital, we weren't sure
   who would keep the baby.

It was the end of summer, and the turtle got out
   of its glass box on the porch.

Children go from womb to temple, but the temple
   goes by other names.

When you make a deal with God, you can't be heavy hearted.

Hannah sewed a robe each year to take to the son she gave away.

She was barefoot.

She wanted the crying to stop, a husband, a night of sleep.

She emptied her breasts at midnight in the hospital sink.

We told our son stories about how it certainly crawled away
   from the road.

Abraham got Isaac back after the test. The boy was
   never his again.

It found its way to the pond by the railroad tracks.

The grandfather held the infant up to the visitor's window
   for her to see.

The deep water would save it from the cold.

Diastasis Recti

Safe to say that life often returns
the vessel broken. To carry
a creature that has been known
to steal the mother's bones for its own.

Muscles of the abdomen, halves
of a zipper never meeting again.
Frequently the woman doesn't notice the gap
or discover it until after the baby learns
to walk and she stands up straight again.

She hides it under her shirts, like a high
school pregnancy. The poets, even they
were ruined after birth. Anne
Bradstreet, and eight children later,
only her couplets resembling her former
body, drawn tight with masculine rhyme.
Sylvia, skinny as a boy, what came
undone by the presence of two lives
within your space?

A cracked cup, a bell rung too soon.
To know God

has loved ruins, has burned out
stars, torn up the skies, ripped the parachutes of autumn
as the mantis hangs six torn veils on the bush
on her way to being a great-eyed priestess.

Finding a Place for It

To move an urn the size of a coin is to move a needle

of a broken compass, the mother like David
building a house for God's law.

North is a guess of the brokenhearted.

One might call it birth, this slow river
that brings the body once the heartbeat folds like a paper boat.

With luck a child grows without leaving his body behind,
fills a man's shoes.

When the unborn forfeits his bones, they become a flower
on the moon, the mother climbing into a rocket.

Tell the older children that small bodies make a smudge of ash
no bigger than the dust a moth shakes off itself.

Certain objects can be hidden in a jewelry box for safekeeping.

The dead never agreed to rest.

Uzzah reached out to steady God's ark and was struck dead.

Set it where everyone can see it
beside the potted fern and the figurines of birds.

The immortal never agreed to be put into statues.

A mother can't stare at a hand forever, no matter
how perfectly the curled fingers would fit into an apostrophe.

At the end of the book, God dwells within us,
and we take our eyes off the temple.

That Slip of Light When Clouds Move Apart Briefly

We wouldn't have investigated the shape in the attic if
    we could endure mystery.

Large headstones are passed on foot like safe neighborhoods.

Because it was dark and didn't sing, we were sure it had sharp teeth.

Small stones are hard to cross in front of. They face strong wind.

The mother tries to memorize her child's features
    before warmth leaves.

It wasn't in our power to imagine a creature with gorgeous feathers.

The funerals are short.

Decades later women talk on porches, and the story slips out
    like a doll from a closet.

We couldn't tolerate the idea of something wild
    tearing through our house.

Not a crocus, which lasts through spring, but a dream flower.

We bought mesh to hang in the threshold of the attic
    to contain the thing.

It disappeared as if it could travel through glass panes.

There is more than one kind of secret death.

It could end with the mother consoled by a people who stop
    to read small stones.

The Spare Room

      You are a child of the grass. What you see are literal things,
two-headed insects landing in the yard, wings like mills of glass.
      The spare room, a closed door at the end
of your grandmother's hall, clean and pink
like the inside of a shell, the bed cover
pulled taut, hand mirror turned from dust
that would collect on your face, wall paper resisting
the decay of hours.
      It's lucky to find shelter when you are young,
before the fear that serenity
would take your life away,
before you've had to go hungry,
before funerals and idols.
      There are few times a person stands
the light, and the motion picture is rare
that critics like—of thousands come from the great ordeal
now at peace. Inconsolable,
we want horse and fire, mad kisses,
the death of birds.
      In a closed room
when you can still smell dew on the breath of summer,
you lie on your back doing nothing.
Two spaces knit together like a double creature
turning in the wind.
You meet the stranger
who keeps you well, endures a calm
that would finish the world.

Laura Cini English grew up in the Northeast, most of her childhood spent in a town that smelled like chocolate. Helping people to write their memoirs both online and in small groups has become her life's passion, and she has learned: "The world is weeds. But when you share a story that changed your life, a flower opens painfully or joyously. And the weeds make room for its beauty." When she's away from things literary, she works in a school feeding children. Her poetry has appeared in various journals and reviews, and at one time, she wrote for a national TV cable guide. She has also worked as a writing tutor, associate editor, and Spanish teacher. She lives in Elizabethtown, PA with her linguist husband and four children. She can be contacted through her website. www.living-muse-with-laura-english.com

www.ingramcontent.com/pod-product-compliance
Lightning Source LLC
LaVergne TN
LVHW041512070426
835507LV00012B/1505